250+ QUESTIONS YOU MAY BE ASKED DURING AN INTERVIEW: PREPARE NOW TO BE READY FOR YOUR NEXT INTERVIEW

Lisa Rusczyk Ed. D.

250+ Questions You May Be Asked During an Interview Copyright © 2018 by CZYK Publishing LLC. All Rights Reserved.

All rights reserved. No part of this book may be reproduced in any form or by any electronic or mechanical means including information storage and retrieval systems, without permission in writing from the author. The only exception is by a reviewer, who may quote short excerpts in a review.

Greater Than a Tourist
Visit our website at www.GreaterThanaTourist.com

Lock Haven, PA
All rights reserved.
ISBN: 9781983088223

BOOK DESCRIPTION

Are you preparing for an interview?

Do you have an interview coming up?

Would you like to know some questions you may be asked or could ask as an interviewer?

There are many types of job questions that you may be asked in any order during an interview. Questions could be about the job itself, the company, the team, feedback, or the next step in the process. Questions could be about salary, career development, personal, career goals, training, or the culture. Remember not only are they interviewing you for the job, they are making sure you are a good fit for the position. They may even ask you brain teaser questions to see how quickly you can think.

Remember you are also interviewing them to make sure you are a good fit for the company and position. There are no right answers to any of these questions.

INTRODUCTION

There are many types of job questions that you may be asked in any order during an interview. Questions could be about the job itself, the company, the team, feedback, or the next step in the process. Questions could be about salary, career development, personal, career goals, training, or the culture. Remember not only are they interviewing you for the job, they are making sure you are a good fit for the position. They may even ask you brain teaser questions to see how quickly you can think. Remember you are also interviewing them to make sure you are a good fit for the company and position. There are no right answers to any of these questions.

ARE YOU...?

- Are you a leader or a follower?

- Are you a self-motivator?

- Are you able to work on several assignments at once?

- Are you interviewing with one of our competitors?

- Are you lucky?

- Are you nice?

- Are you overqualified for this job?

- Are you willing to relocate?

- Are you willing to travel?

- Are you willing to work flextime?

DESCRIBE...?

- Describe a difficult work situation and how you overcame it?

- Describe a situation at a past job where you had to take initiative?

- Describe a time when your workload was heavy and how you handled it?

- Describe a time where you made a major mistake and had to think on your feet to come up with a solution?

- Describe failure?

- Describe how you managed a problem employee?

- Describe how you would handle a situation if you were required to finish multiple tasks by the end of the day, and there was no conceivable way that you could finish them?

- Describe success?

- Describe the gap in your employment history?

- Describe your educational background?

- Describe your ideal boss?

- Describe your ideal job?

- Describe your resume?

- Describe your work style?

- Describe yourself?

HAVE YOU EVER...?

- Have you ever been fired from a previous position?

- Have you ever been on a team where someone was not pulling their own weight? How did you handle it?

- Have you ever done any volunteer work? What kind?

- Have you ever had any failures? What did you learn from them?

- Have you ever had difficulty getting along with a former professor/ supervisor/ coworker and how did you handle it?

- Have you ever had difficulty working with a manager?

- Have you ever managed employees before?

- Have you ever mentored an employee to help achieve their career goals?

- Have you ever quit a job? Why?

- Have you ever spoken before a group of people? How large?

- Have you ever worked with someone who did

  not like your work?

HOW DO YOU...?

- How do you envision this position supporting you?

- How do you evaluate success?

- How do you feel about creativity and individuality?

- How do you feel about taking no for an answer?

- How do you feel about the possibility of relocating?

- How do you feel about travel?
- How do you feel about working in a structured environment?
- How do you feel about working overtime?
- How do you handle a customer negative review on the company facebook page?
- How do you handle failure?
- How do you handle pressure?
- How do you handle stress?
- How do you handle success?
- How do you plan to achieve goals?

- How do you think I rate as an interviewer?

- How do you view yourself?

- How do you want to improve yourself in the next year?

How Would You...?

- How would you adjust to working for a new company?

- How would you deal with an angry or irate customer?

- How would you describe the pace at which you work?

- How would you describe your management style?

- How would you describe your work style?

- How would you describe yourself?

- How would you feel about working for a younger manager?
- How would you feel about working for someone who knows less than you?
- How would you fire someone?
- How would you go about establishing your credibility quickly with the team?
- How would you weigh a plane without scales?

IF...?

- If I called your boss right now and asked him what is an area that you could improve on, what would he say?

- If I were your supervisor and asked you to do something that you disagreed with, what would you do?

- If you could be anywhere in the world right now, where would you be?

- If you could choose one superhero power, what would it be and why?
- If you could get rid of any one of the US states, which one would you get rid of and why?
- If you could talk with any one person, whom would it be and why?
- If you know your boss is 100% wrong about something how would you handle it?
- If you were an animal, which one would you want to be?

- If you were to start over, what would you change about your education?

Tell me...

- Tell me 10 ways to use a pencil other than writing.

- Tell me a past situation where you had to work with colleagues or team members who were very different from you.

- Tell me about a past situation where you had to juggle multiple projects with competing deadlines.

- Tell me about a time when you disagreed with your boss.

- Tell me about a time when you had to give someone difficult feedback. How did you handle it?
- Tell me about a time when you received criticism and how you reacted to it.
- Tell me about a time where you had to deal with conflict on the job.
- Tell me about a time where you had to put in significant effort up front and then wait a long time for success.
- Tell me about a time you made a mistake.

- Tell me about an accomplishment you are most proud of.

- Tell me about how you handled a situation where you had to work with a difficult colleague.

- Tell me about something that is not on your resume.

- Tell me about something you would have done differently at work.

- Tell me about the project you are most proud of from your past work history.

- Tell me about your proudest achievement.

- Tell me about yourself.

- Tell me an assignment was too difficult for you, and how did you resolve the issue.

- Tell me five words that describe your character.

- Tell me how frequently is formal reviews given to new employees.

- Tell me how long have you worked in the industry.

- Tell me how long will it take for you to make a significant contribution in this position.

- Tell me how long you worked at your last job.

- Tell me how many times does a clock's hands overlap in a day.

- Tell me how this job fits in with your career plan.

- Tell me how will your greatest strength help you perform. In which campus activities did you participate?

- Tell me how you rate me as an interviewer.

- Tell me how you would sell me this pencil.
- Tell me the difference between good and exceptional.
- Tell me the way you learned about this position.
- Tell me three accomplishments that you are most proud.
- Tell me what attracted you to this company.
- Tell me what challenges you are looking for in a position.

- Tell me what did you like or dislike about your previous job.

- Tell me what events have been crucial in your life.

- Tell me what excites you about coming into work.

- Tell me what gets you most excited about the company's future.

- Tell me what gets you up in the morning.

- Tell me what has been your most successful campaign in the past.

- Tell me what has been your proudest achievement so far.

- Tell me what interests you about this job.

- Tell me what irritates you about other people, and how do you deal with it.

- Tell me what you can contribute to this company.

- Tell me what you have been doing since your last job.

- Tell me what you have learned from these work experiences.

- Tell me when the last time you were angry was. What happened?

- Tell me when you could start work.

- Tell me when you were most satisfied in your job.

- Tell me where else are you interviewing.

- Tell me where you want to be in five years. Ten years.

- Tell me where you went to school.

- Tell me where you would like to be in your career five years from now.

- Tell me which classes in your major did you like the best.

- Tell me which elective classes did you like best in college. Least? Why?

- Tell me you can do better for us than the other candidates for the job.

- With your eyes closed, tell me step-by-step how to tie my shoes.

What Are...?

- What are the qualities of a bad leader?

- What are the qualities of a good leader?

- What are three positive character traits you do not have?

- What are three positive things your last boss would say about you?

- What are three things your former manager would like you to improve on?

- What are you looking for in terms of career development?

- What are you looking for in your next job?

- What are you most proud of?

- What are you passionate about?

- What are your career goals?

- What are your hobbies?

- What are your lifelong dreams?

- What are your pet peeves?

- What are your salary requirements?

- What are your strengths?

- What are your weaknesses?

What do you ...?

- What do you do in your spare time?

- What do you do to stay up to date with new marketing techniques?

- What do you expect from a supervisor?

- What do you find are the most difficult decisions to make?

- What do you know about this company?

- What do you know about this industry?

- What do you like the most and least about working in this industry?

- What do you like to do for fun?

- What do you see ahead for the company in the next five years?

- What do you see yourself doing within the first 30 days of this job?

- What do you think are the most enjoyable or gratifying aspects for someone in this role?

- What do you think of your previous boss?

- What do you ultimately want to become?

What is...?

- What is different about working here than anywhere else You have worked?

- What is good customer service?

- What is the background of the company?

- What is the best movie you have seen in the last year?

- What is the biggest criticism you received from your boss?

- What is the last book you read?

- What is the most challenging thing for you to get used to in this position?

- What is the most difficult decision you have made in the last two years and how did you come to that decision?

- What is the most important thing you have learned in high school?

- What is the most important thing you learned in school?

- What is the name of our CEO?

- What is the salary range?

- What is the worst thing that you have ever gotten away with?

- What is your availability?

- What is your biggest regret and why?

- What is your company's market or target demographic?

- What is your dream job?

- What is your favorite memory from childhood?

- What is your favorite office tradition?

- What is your favorite website?

- What is your greatest achievement outside of work?
- What is your greatest failure, and what did you learn from it?
- What is your greatest fear?
- What is your ideal company?
- What is your ideal work environment?
- What is your personal mission statement?
- What is your professional development plan?
- What is your salary history?

What...?

- What kind of boss do you prefer?

- What kind of goals would you have in mind if you got this job?

- What kind of personality do you work best with and why?

- What kinds of processes are in place to help me work collaboratively?

- What magazines do you subscribe to?

- What major challenges and problems did you face? How did you handle them?

- What makes you angry?

- What makes you uncomfortable?

- What mark do you feel You have left on your school?

- What marketing strategies do you prefer to use?

- What metrics or goals will my performance be evaluated against?

- What motivates you most in a job?

- What motivates you?

- What negative thing would your last boss say about you?

- What new product lines/services have been announced recently?

- What opportunities will there be to work with new, interesting technologies?

- What other types of positions are you considering?

- What part of the job will be the least challenging for you?

- What particular aspects about my background and experience interest you?

- What particular computer equipment and software do you use?

- What philosophy guides your work?

- What problems have you encountered at work?

- What questions do you have for me?

- What questions haven't I asked you?

- What recently-developed marketing strategy, technique or tool interests you the most right now?

- What strategies would you use to motivate your team?

- What strength will help you the most to succeed?

- What techniques and tools do you use to keep yourself organized?

- What three character traits would your friends use to describe you?

- What type of animal are you?
- What type of work environment do you prefer?
- What was the last book you have read for fun?
- What was the last project you headed up, and what was its outcome?
- What was the most difficult period in your life, and how did you deal with it?
- What was your biggest failure?
- What were the responsibilities of your last position?

- What were your responsibilities?

- What will you do if you do not get this position?

- What will you miss most about your last job?

- What would be your ideal company culture?

- What job-related skills have you developed?

What would ...?

- What would be your ideal working environment?

- What would you consider to be the most important aspects of this job?

- What would you do if you found out the company was doing something illegal?

- What would you do if you won the lottery?

- What would you look to accomplish in the first 30 days on the job?

- What would you say is the most important aspect of our company culture?

- What would your past managers say about you?

Who....

- Who are your heroes?

- Who are your role models?

- Who do you compare yourself to?

- Who has impacted you most in your career and how?

- Who is your mentor?

- Who was your favorite manager and why?

Why....

- Why are you interested in a no management job?

- Why are you interested in taking a lower level job?

- Why are you looking for a new job?

- Why are you the best person for the job?

- Why did you choose to attend your college or university?

- Why did you choose to interview with our organization?

- Why did you choose your major?

- Why did you come to this company?

- Why did you go back to school?

- Why did you quit your job?

- Why did you resign?

- Why do you want this job?

- Why do you want to change jobs?

- Why do you want to leave your current company?

- Why do you want to work here?

- Why have you been out of work so long?

- Why is there fuzz on a tennis ball?

- Why should I take a risk on you?

- Why should we hire you?

- Why shouldn't we hire you?

- Why was there a gap in your employment?

- Why were you fired?

- Why were you laid off?

- Why weren't you promoted at your last job?

- Why would you take a job for less money?

You have...?

- You have been put in charge of planning the company's nationwide conference? Where do you begin?

- You have been tasked with redesigning the company's brand strategy from the ground up? Walk me through your process?

- You have just picked up a call from a customer who claims to have not received his shipment, even though UPS confirms it was delivered? What do you do?

Would you....

- Would you be successful working with a team?

- Would you consider relocating?

- Would you consider traveling for this position?

- Would you consider yourself a big picture person?

- Would you consider yourself a detail oriented person?

- Would you work 40+ hours a week?

NOTES

www.ingramcontent.com/pod-product-compliance
Lightning Source LLC
Chambersburg PA
CBHW030503220526
45464CB00006B/2638